A Kid's Guide to
BACKYARD BIRDS

Eliza Berkowitz

illustrated by
Nicole LaRue

Gibbs Smith

INTRODUCTION

Whether you have been interested in birds for a long time or are just starting to appreciate our feathered friends, it's easy to become a bird-watcher!

There are three very simple steps to basic birding:

1. GO OUTSIDE
2. KEEP YOUR EYES PEELED
3. KEEP YOUR EARS OPEN

Every time you leave your house, there are opportunities to spot birds. On your walk to the school bus? Birds are flying between the trees! Playing catch in your backyard? Birds are building a nest in a shrub! Outside at recess? Birds are hopping in the grass looking for earthworms (or leftover bits of your lunch)! Birds are everywhere, and once you take the time to look for them, you'll be surprised by how many birds you see (or hear!) in a day.

This book will get you familiar with the 40 birds you're most likely to see in the United States year-round. You'll learn what they eat, what they use to build their nests, and so much more. In a banner at the top of each page, you'll even get to learn their common name *and* their scientific, also known as their Latin name! At the back of the book, there's a bird log to help you keep track of all the birds you have spotted and a glossary where you can find definitions of words found throughout the text. How many of the birds in this book can you find?

The beauty of birding is that anyone can do it. You don't need any fancy equipment to get started. The more time you spend outside, the more birds you'll see. And the more birds you see, the more you will come to appreciate the wonders of these special creatures!

DIY PROJECT

The best way to attract birds to your backyard is to offer them a delicious homemade treat. Making your own bird feeders is easy and fun. Here's a basic recipe that will attract many different types of birds to your yard.

APPLE

TWINE

First, cut the **apple** in half lengthwise. Use your **spoon** to scoop out the seeds from both halves. In a bowl, mix the **sunflower seeds** and **millet**. Spread the **peanut butter** on each apple half. Then press the halves into the sunflower seed and millet mixture. The peanut butter should help everything stick together. With an adult's help, make a hole at the top of each apple half and slip through a piece of **twine**. Tie a knot to join the ends of the twine, and you're done!

You now have two bird feeders. Hang them on trees and enjoy the sights and sounds that they bring to your yard.

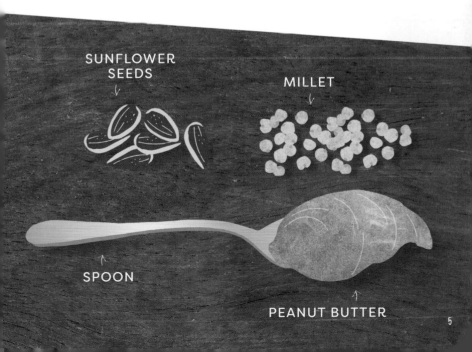

SUNFLOWER
SEEDS

MILLET

SPOON

PEANUT BUTTER

IDENTIFICATION

There are four main ways to identify types of birds. Become familiar with the clues below to become an ID expert.

GREAT BLUE HERON ↘

AMERICAN GOLDFINCH ↓

RED-BELLIED WOODPECKER ↘

Look at a bird's **size** and **shape**. Knowing the size of a bird can help point you in the right direction. Get familiar with the size of birds common to your area. Now observe whether the bird you're looking to ID is larger or smaller than these common birds. You can also use the size and shape of a bird's features to help identify it. Check out the beak, tail, and wings. Look for signs that point to one type of bird over another.

A bird's **color pattern** is another good way to identify it. Pay attention to the overall color of the bird. Do you see any other colors? When the bird flies, is the underwing color different from the rest of the bird? Does it have any special markings on its head or face?

A bird's **behavior** will also give you important clues. Can you observe what a bird is eating or how it is looking for food? Can you spot its nest and see what materials were used to build it? Is it loud or quiet? Does it seem to be alone or with other birds of the same type?

You should also consider the **habitat** where you've spotted a bird. Is it in an area with a lot of trees or is it more open? Is there water nearby? Are there large grassy areas? Also take notice of its **range** since some birds are seen in different areas at different points in the season.

There's a lot to learn when it comes to identifying birds, but starting with these clues will make you a pro in no time.

WHAT'S IN MY BAG?

When you first go out looking for birds, you don't need to bring anything special. Simply observe the sights and sounds. Look up and take notice of the birds you see. Pay attention to their colors, shapes, and sizes. Look at the way they flap their wings when they fly. As you become more experienced in the art of bird-watching, there are a few things that may be helpful to have:

Binoculars will help you see details from a distance. You can get a closer look at a bird in its natural environment without disturbing it by being too close.

A **camera** is nice to have. When you take photos, you can go back and zoom in to see any details you may have missed. Or you may just want to save them as a reminder of the birds you've seen!

If you're heading into a wooded area, **bug spray** will keep the insects away. You don't want to be distracted by a bug bite when there's a pair of goldfinches making a nest in a nearby tree!

Sneakers or **hiking boots** will keep your feet comfy if you're doing a lot of walking. When you're travelling on uneven ground, like in a wooded area, proper footwear can also prevent injuries.

Keep a **notebook** and **pen** handy. You never know when you might see an unusual bird and want to jot down its features or behaviors.

And finally, don't forget **this book** to help you identify the birds you come across!

NORTHERN CARDINAL

Cardinalis cardinalis

When you spot a bright red Northern Cardinal, you can be sure it's a male. The female is more of a grayish color, with some red in its wing feathers and a red-tipped **crest**. Cardinals are known for their sweet singing. They are also known to be tough. The males will attack any bird that threatens their territory.

NEST

They build their nests in trees or shrubs, about 1 to 15 feet high. They use twigs, leaves, bark, grasses, stems, and small roots to build their nests (which are only 2 to 3 inches tall!).

FOOD

Northern Cardinals eat fruits, including wild grapes and blackberries. They also eat seeds (sunflower seeds are their favorite) and many kinds of insects, including centipedes and katydids.

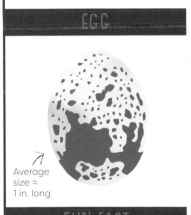

YEAR-ROUND

HABITAT & RANGE

Cardinals live in a variety of **habitats**. They look for areas that are thick with shrubs and **foliage**. They used to be found only in warmer climates, but are now spotted all over the eastern United States.

EGG

↗
Average
size =
1 in. long

FUN FACT

These seven U.S. states call the Northern Cardinal their state bird: Illinois, Indiana, Kentucky, North Carolina, Ohio, Virginia, and West Virginia.

MOURNING DOVE

Zenaida macroura

Have you ever looked up and seen a grayish brown bird perched on a telephone wire? There's a good chance you've spotted a Mourning Dove! They are one of the most common birds, with about 350 million in the United States alone.

NEST

These birds are not picky about where to build a nest. In a tree, they may choose a spot that's hidden by leaves. But they also build nests on other structures and even on the ground. They use pine needles, twigs, and grass to build their fragile nests.

FOOD

Mourning Doves eat mostly seeds—lots and lots of them! About 1% of their diet comes from other foods, like grasses and berries.

YEAR-ROUND

HABITAT & RANGE

Mourning Doves are found all over the United States. They prefer open areas with some trees.

EGG

↗
Average
size =
1 in. long

FUN FACT

A Mourning Dove stores seeds in a little patch inside its throat called a **crop**. It's not unusual for them to gather thousands of seeds in their crop before flying to a safe place to digest them.

I WHISTLE!

SIZE

Length: 8 to 11 inches
Wingspan: 12 to 16 inches

AMERICAN ROBIN

Turdus migratorius

It's true what they say—the early bird gets the worm! In the early mornings, robins can be found waiting patiently on lawns for worms to pop up. They begin their musical chirping about an hour before the sun rises. If you begin to see robins at the end of winter, that's a sure sign that spring is on its way.

NEST

Robins build their nests on different structures. They might choose the outside of a house or a shed, or they might choose a tree, where they can hide beneath leaves. Female robins use twigs and dead grass to form a cup shape. Mud is used to make the nest strong. Thin pieces of dry grass are added inside to create a soft padding for the eggs.

FOOD

The American Robin's favorite food is earthworms. They also enjoy fruit.

■ YEAR-ROUND

HABITAT & RANGE

American Robins are common all over the United States. You can find them in backyards, parks, and fields. They are also found in more wild areas, like forests and **woodlands**.

EGG

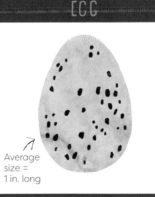

↗
Average size = 1 in. long

FUN FACT

"Robin's egg blue" is a well-known shade of blue.

15

AMERICAN CROW

Corvus brachyrhynchos

Often seen in large **flocks** of hundreds (or even thousands!), the American Crow is recognizable by its all-black appearance. Crows are known for being curious and smart. They can be very clever when it comes to finding food. It's not unusual for a crow to steal from another bird or catch a fish to eat!

NEST

Crows' nests are sturdy. Built in treetops, they are usually made from dead branches, bark, weeds, and mud. Nests are lined with softer materials, like grass and feathers.

FOOD

Crows are not picky. They eat almost anything! They enjoy worms, seeds, fruit, and insects, but they will also eat garbage and dead animals (also called **carrion**).

YEAR-ROUND

HABITAT & RANGE

American Crows are found throughout the United States. They are very common in cities and suburban areas.

EGG

↗ Average size = 1½ in. long

FUN FACT

A group of crows is called a murder.

BLUE JAY

Cyanocitta cristata

Blue Jays are one of the most eye-catching birds. Their bright blue feathers make them easy to spot. Even if you don't see them, you will hear them! Their calls can sometimes be loud, even though their songs are often quiet. They have been known to mimic the calls of hawks. They are intelligent and have close family ties.

NEST

These birds like to make their nests in the outer branches of a tree, about 10 to 25 feet high. They use fresh twigs and small roots to make their nests. They may also use grass and mud.

FOOD

Blue Jays are known for their love of acorns. They also eat insects, nuts, and seeds.

YEAR-ROUND

HABITAT & RANGE

Blue Jays are drawn to oak trees. There are usually more oaks at the edges of forests, so that is a good place to find them. They are often seen in urban and suburban areas, where bird feeders make it easy to find food. They are found in most of the United States except the Southwest.

EGG

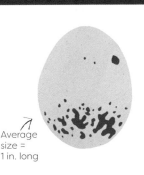

↗ Average size = 1 in. long

FUN FACT

Blue Jays often mate for life. They stick with their partner until one of them dies. Only then will a Blue Jay look for another mate.

19

SONG SPARROW

Melospiza melodia

One of the most common sparrows in the United States, the Song Sparrow can vary in color and size. In the southwestern United States, Song Sparrows are lighter in color. As you head north, they tend to be darker. In parts of Alaska, the Song Sparrow is dark brown.

NEST

Together, a pair of Song Sparrows will look for a place to nest. They like to hide their nests in areas of thick grasses or weeds, often pretty low to the ground. The female uses loose grass, bark, and weeds to form the outside of the cup-shaped nest. Then she lines the inside with more grass, small roots, and animal hair.

FOOD

Seeds and fruit are a staple of the Song Sparrow's diet. In the summer, they eat lots of insects, including grasshoppers and snails.

■ **YEAR-ROUND**

HABITAT & RANGE

Song Sparrows are found all over the United States. They thrive in many different open **habitats**. They are not afraid of humans, so you will find many in the suburbs.

EGG

↗ Average size = 1 in. long

FUN FACT

Often when you hear a Song Sparrow, it is a male bird. They use singing to attract a mate and to scare away predators.

21

CONK-LA-REE!

SIZE

Length: 7 to 9 inches
Wingspan: 12 to 16 inches

RED-WINGED BLACKBIRD

Agelaius phoeniceus

Male and female Red-Winged Blackbirds look very different from one another. The males are glossy black with red and yellow feathers on their shoulders. The females are more of a patterned brown color with a touch of orange on their shoulders. You can often find them in large **flocks** with other blackbirds and starlings.

NEST

The female Red-Winged Blackbird builds the nest. She weaves stringy plant material around stems, then adds wet leaves, dead pieces of wood, and mud. Inside, she lays down dry grass.

FOOD

During the summer months, Red-Winged Blackbirds eat mostly insects. In the winter, they eat mostly seeds.

■ **YEAR-ROUND**

HABITAT & RANGE

These birds prefer wetter environments. You can find them in freshwater and saltwater marshes or in areas with wet roadsides. There are lots of them all over the United States.

EGG

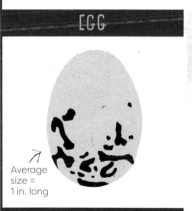

↗
Average size = 1 in. long

FUN FACT

Red-Winged Blackbirds prefer to feed on the ground. If you want to attract them to your yard, try spreading seed and grain on the ground instead of putting it inside a feeder.

23

AMERICAN GOLDFINCH

Spinus tristis

The American Goldfinch is known for its eye-catching feathers. In the warmer months, they are bright yellow and black with white streaks on their wings and tails. In the winter, their feathers fade to brown. You can easily tell the males from the females. The males have brighter feathers and a black spot on their foreheads.

NEST

To build their nests, goldfinches weave together small roots and bits of plant material. Their nests can be so tightly woven that they hold water. They also use spider silk to make a soft lining in their nests. Spider silk is the hairlike wisps that make up spiderwebs!

FOOD

Goldfinches are vegetarians and they eat mostly seeds. (But they may accidentally eat an insect from time to time.)

YEAR-ROUND

HABITAT & RANGE

American Goldfinches live all over the United States. They avoid deep forests and prefer open areas. They are drawn to backyards all over the continent to visit bird feeders.

EGG

↗ Average size = 1½ in. long

FUN FACT

American Goldfinches change color twice a year. They do this by shedding their feathers and growing new ones, a process called **molting**.

I IMITATE!

SIZE

Length: 8 to 9 inches
Wingspan: 12 to 16 inches

EUROPEAN STARLING

Sturnus vulgaris

European Starlings are easiest to spot in the warmer months. In spring and summer, they sport dark iridescent feathers that look green and purple in bright light. Their coloring helps them attract a mate before **breeding** season. In the cooler months, they take on a less flashy look, with brown feathers that show spots of white.

HABITAT & RANGE

Starlings live in towns and cities throughout much of the United States. They like to be near open, grassy fields. There, they can look for food. They often use man-made structures for nesting purposes.

NEST

European Starlings will look for a hole about 10 to 25 feet high in which to nest. It could be a hole in a tree left by a woodpecker, but it's often an empty space or gap in a building or streetlight. The nest is built on a base of grass and pine needles, with feathers, bits of string, and other trash.

EGG

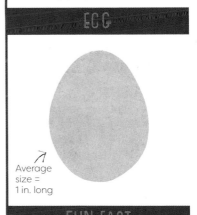

↗ Average size = 1 in. long

FOOD

They prefer to eat insects such as grasshoppers, caterpillars, and spiders, but they will eat almost anything, including fruit, seeds, and even garbage.

FUN FACT

European Starlings did not exist in the United States until 1890. At that time, 60 birds were brought from Europe and set free in Central Park. Now there are over 200 million!

CHEEP!

SIZE

Length: 5 to 5½ inches
Wingspan: 8 to 10 inches

HOUSE FINCH

Haemorhous mexicanus

Cheerful and cute, the House Finch is a familiar sight at bird feeders across the United States. You will rarely see just one—it's more likely you'll see groups of these social birds looking for food together. You can recognize the males by the red coloring on their faces and upper breast. The females are harder to identify, with streaky gray and brown coloring.

NEST

A pair of House Finches will choose a site for their nest together. The female then builds the nest using grass, weeds, thin twigs, leaves, small roots, and sometimes feathers or string. Nests are often built in trees, but it's not unusual to find one in a planter, windowsill, or streetlamp.

FOOD

House Finches enjoy seeds, flower parts, berries, fruit, and the occasional insect. They are known to visit backyard bird feeders, and they especially love sunflower seeds.

■ **YEAR-ROUND**

HABITAT & RANGE

They are native to the southeastern United States. They were introduced to the East Coast in 1939 and quickly multiplied. They now live in almost every state. They live in cities, towns, and suburbs.

EGG

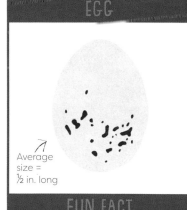

↗ Average size = ½ in. long

FUN FACT

House Finches have been known to steal sugar water from hummingbird feeders!

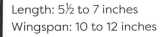

Length: 5½ to 7 inches
Wingspan: 10 to 12 inches

DOWNY WOODPECKER

Dryobates pubescens

Downy Woodpeckers are frequently confused with Hairy Woodpeckers. The two look almost identical, but their size gives them away. Downy Woodpeckers are much smaller. In fact, they are the smallest type of woodpecker. Of all the woodpeckers, they are the most likely to show up at your bird feeder.

NEST

They nest in trees that are dead (or that have dead parts). The softer wood makes it easier for the woodpecker to make a hole. Once the hole is large enough, they line it with wood chips to make a nest.

FOOD

They eat mostly insects, including ants and caterpillars. About a quarter of their diet comes from plants, such as berries and grains. Downy Woodpeckers are not shy about visiting a bird feeder, especially if it has **suet**.

■ **YEAR-ROUND**

HABITAT & RANGE

Downy Woodpeckers prefer to live in forests. They can also be found in suburbs, parks, and other open areas with trees nearby. They are the most widespread woodpecker and live throughout the United States.

EGG

↗ Average size = 1 in. long

FUN FACT

The Downy Woodpecker's superfast drumming clocks in at 17 beats per second.

CANADA GOOSE

Branta canadensis

Canada Geese are big, social birds. Most of the year, they stay with a large **flock**, usually made up of birds they're related to. They mate for life and will break off into pairs in the spring to have baby geese (also called goslings). They are known for being mean to any bird (or human!) that threatens their territory.

NEST

They build nests close to the ground, usually near water. They use dry grass, moss, and other plant matter to form the base of their nest. The female waits for the second egg to be laid, then adds feathers to the inside of the nest.

FOOD

In warmer months, Canada Geese eat mostly grass. In cooler months, they rely on berries and seeds. They are known to be fond of blueberries and corn.

■ **YEAR-ROUND**

HABITAT & RANGE

Canada Geese live in areas where they can find both water and open grassy fields. They're found all over the United States.

EGG

↗
Average size = 3½ in. long

FUN FACT

The oldest known Canada Goose was at least 33 years old!

MALLARD

Anas platyrhynchos

If you've ever gone to a park to feed ducks, you have likely seen a Mallard. The most common of all ducks, they can be found wherever there is water, such as lakes, ponds, and even sometimes in swimming pools! Males have green heads and yellow beaks. Females are mostly brown with a brownish orange bill.

NEST

Mallards make their nests on the ground. The female Mallard pulls grass, twigs, and leaves from nearby. She often uses other greenery to hide herself and the nest. Once she has laid eggs, she will pull her own feathers out to cover them.

FOOD

Mallards are dabbling ducks. That means they do not dive in water for food. Instead, they tip forward to snack on plants below the surface. They also look for worms, snails, and shrimp to eat. On land, they eat a varied diet. They may pick at plant matter or accept bits of bread from humans.

■ **YEAR-ROUND**

HABITAT & RANGE

Mallards are found primarily in North America and Europe, but there are also populations in South Africa, New Zealand, Asia, and Australia.

EGG

↗
Average size = 2½ in. long

FUN FACT

At the end of their **breeding** season, Mallards will lose their flight feathers. This will make them unable to fly for 3 to 4 weeks!

35

RED-BELLIED WOODPECKER

Melanerpes carolinus

Despite their name, Red-Bellied Woodpeckers don't have red bellies. They do, however, have a bright red streak on their heads. These noisy birds can often be found pecking at bark or flying in an up and down pattern, like a roller coaster.

NEST

A Red-Bellied Woodpecker pecks away at the soft wood of dead trees to create a hidden hole in which to nest. They lay down wood chips, and there, the female bird lays her eggs.

FOOD

These birds eat a wide variety of foods. They eat insects and spiders, as well as plants, seeds, and fruits. If you want to draw them to your bird feeder, try adding **suet** and peanuts.

■ YEAR-ROUND

HABITAT & RANGE

Red-Bellied Woodpeckers live in the eastern United States. They mostly live in forests and wooded suburbs.

EGG

↗
Average size = 1 in. long

FUN FACT

Red-Bellied Woodpeckers have long, sticky tongues! They use them to catch prey.

SIZE

Length: 5 to 6 inches
Wingspan: 6 to 8 inches

BLACK-CAPPED CHICKADEE

Poecile atricapillus

When you first see a Black-Capped Chickadee, you may squeal with delight at its cuteness! These little **songbirds** are frequent visitors to bird feeders, but they don't stick around for long. They will grab their food and fly away to eat it elsewhere or hide it for later.

NEST

Male and female chickadees search for a nesting site together. Sometimes they use a hole left behind by another bird. Other times they peck away at rotten wood to create a new hole. Inside, the female builds the nest. She uses moss for the base and soft materials, such as rabbit fur, on the inside.

FOOD

They eat lots of seeds, berries, plants, spiders, insects, and even bits of fat and meat from the remains of dead animals.

■ **YEAR-ROUND**

HABITAT & RANGE

You can find these adorable birds in the northern United States. They can be found anywhere there are trees or woody shrubs to nest in.

EGG

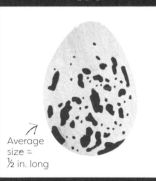

↗ Average size = ½ in. long

FUN FACT

Black-Capped Chickadees will hide food to save it for later. They can remember thousands of hiding places!

39

CHEEP!

SIZE

Length: 6 to 7 inches
Wingspan: 7½ to 10 inches

HOUSE SPARROW

Passer domesticus

House Sparrows are one of the most common birds. They live alongside humans in cities and towns. You can easily lure these small brown **songbirds** to your yard with a bird feeder or by scattering seeds on the ground. Some may even eat out of your hand!

NEST

House Sparrows build nests inside of holes and spaces they find. They prefer nesting in man-made structures, like the roof of a house or barn. When they find a space they like, they stuff the hole with dried plant matter. Then, using softer materials, such as feathers and paper, they create a lining on which to lay their eggs.

FOOD

They eat mostly seeds and are happy to eat from bird feeders. They especially like millet, sunflower seeds, and corn. In the summer, they also eat insects and feed them to their young.

■ **YEAR-ROUND**

HABITAT & RANGE

House Sparrows are found throughout the world. In the United States, they live everywhere except Alaska. They live in cities, towns, and suburbs—anywhere there are humans.

EGG

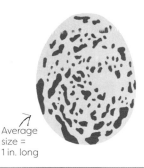

↗ Average size = 1 in. long

FUN FACT

House Sparrows bathe in dirt! They will find soil and dust and rub it over themselves, just as if they were bathing in water.

SIZE

Length: 25 to 32 inches
Wingspan: 67 to 70 inches

TURKEY VULTURE

Cathartes aura

Don't be fooled—the Turkey Vulture is not a turkey at all! Often seen on roadsides, in farm fields, and at garbage dumps, these predator birds swoop in when an animal has died to eat the remains. They are nature's cleanup crew!

NEST

Turkey Vultures have unusual nesting habits. Unlike other large birds, they do not choose to build a nest high in a tree. Instead, they lay their eggs on the ground or tucked away inside a dark hole.

FOOD

Turkey Vultures are scavengers, meaning they feed on whatever they can find. They will eat almost anything, including garbage. But their favorite meal is **carrion**.

YEAR-ROUND

HABITAT & RANGE

They live all over the United States, but the birds that live in the southern United States will stay all year long. Others will **migrate** south, to Central America and South America.

EGG

↗ Average size = 3 in. long

FUN FACT

Turkey Vultures have an excellent sense of smell. While flying, they can sniff out their next meal from over a mile away.

TUFTED TITMOUSE

Baeolophus bicolor

The Tufted Titmouse is easily identified by its unique pointed **crest**. With gray feathers down its back, a white front, and a light reddish on its sides, it stands out from other kinds of birds in a **flock**.

NEST

Tufted Titmice nest in cavities. They cannot, however, dig the holes themselves. Instead, they depend on the cavities left by woodpeckers. Inside, they use leaves, grass, moss, and bark to build a nest. They line it with hair and fur, some of which is pulled directly from an animal's body!

FOOD

In the warmer months, Tufted Titmice eat mostly bugs, like caterpillars, stink bugs, and ants, as well as spiders and snails. They also enjoy berries, nuts, and seeds. In the winter, they are often seen at bird feeders.

YEAR-ROUND

HABITAT & RANGE

Tufted Titmice live in the eastern United States. You can find them in forests, woods, parks, and suburban neighborhoods where there are lots of trees.

EGG

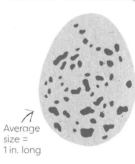

Average size = 1 in. long

FUN FACT

When choosing a seed to eat, they will look for the largest one. They'll carry it away, then hold it with their feet while they hammer away at the shell with their beak.

45

SIZE

Length: 5½ to 6 inches
Wingspan: 7 to 10 inches

DARK-EYED JUNCO

Junco hyemalis

Dark-Eyed Juncos spend a lot of time on the ground, hopping around on the forest floor looking for seeds. Depending on the region, the Dark-Eyed Junco will look a bit different. In the eastern United States, they are more of a gray color. In the western United States, they are more brown, with black on their heads and upper breast.

NEST

Dark-Eyed Juncos prefer to build their nests close to the ground (or even underground!). On the ground, a nest could just be a spot with grasses or pine needles. But they also build sturdy nests with a base of twigs, leaves, and moss lined with grasses, rootlets, and hair.

FOOD

Most of their diet is made up of seeds. During the **breeding** season, they also eat insects, such as butterflies, beetles, and flies.

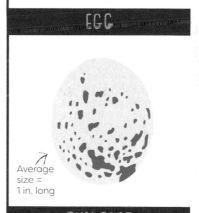

■ **YEAR-ROUND**

HABITAT & RANGE

They are found in wooded areas throughout most of the United States. Your best bet for spotting one is to keep your eyes on the ground, where you may see one hopping around, looking for food.

EGG

↗ Average size = 1 in. long

FUN FACT

Dark-Eyed Juncos are one of the most common birds. The estimated total population is 630 million!

WHA-WHA-WHA!

SIZE

Length: 5 to 5½ inches
Wingspan: 8 to 10½ inches

WHITE-BREASTED NUTHATCH

Sitta carolinensis

The White-Breasted Nuthatch is a small but very loud bird that spends much of its time climbing up and down trees, looking for insects. The name "nuthatch" comes from its unusual way of eating. When it finds a large seed or acorn, it crams it into the bark of a tree. It then uses its sharp bill to "hatch" the seed inside.

NEST

They build their nests in holes they find. The female puts fur, bark, and dirt at the bottom of the hole. She then builds a nest on top of that using bark and softer materials, like feathers and grass.

FOOD

These birds love to eat insects, such as ants, beetles, and caterpillars. Most of their diet comes from insects, but they also eat seeds and nuts. They especially enjoy being served sunflower seeds and peanuts at a bird feeder.

■ YEAR-ROUND

HABITAT & RANGE

The White-Breasted Nuthatch lives in most parts of the United States. They live in forests, parks, and backyards that have large trees.

EGG

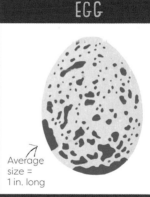

Average size = 1 in. long

FUN FACT

They are known as the "upside-down bird" because of the way they walk upside down as they move down a tree.

NORTHERN FLICKER

Colaptes auratus

The Northern Flicker is a type of woodpecker. Although it is able to hammer away high up in trees, it prefers to hang out on the ground. This is where it gets most of its food. If you spot one, try to catch a glimpse of it in flight. When Northern Flickers spread their wings to fly, they have either bright red or yellow flight feathers.

NEST

Northern Flickers nest in holes. They either chip away at diseased wood to create the hole or reuse a space left by another bird. They line the bottom of the space with wood chips to make a bed for eggs and, eventually, chicks.

FOOD

They eat mostly ants and beetles. In the winter, they may also eat wild fruits and nuts. Although they are not really known to visit bird feeders, adding a bird bath to your yard may attract them.

■ **YEAR-ROUND**

HABITAT & RANGE

Northern Flickers are the most widespread woodpecker in the United States. They like **woodland** areas and open fields with trees scattered about.

EGG

↗ Average size = 1 in. long

FUN FACT

They use their extra-long, sticky tongues to poke into anthills and pick up lots of ants.

CAROLINA WREN

Thryothorus ludovicianus

The Carolina Wren is known for being small but quite noisy. The males sing almost constantly. Following the sound of its singing is a great way to catch a glimpse of these pretty **songbirds**, as they like to stay hidden among the plants and trees.

NEST

Their nests are detailed, made with a variety of materials, such as bark, dead leaves, feathers, straw, paper, and string. Often built with a dome covering and a side entrance, the nests are built by both the males and the females.

FOOD

They consume a little bit of fruit and seeds, but mostly eat spiders and insects. Their diet includes stick bugs, grasshoppers, and cockroaches. They will sometimes eat tree frogs and small lizards too!

YEAR-ROUND

HABITAT & RANGE

Carolina Wrens live mostly in the eastern United States. Being shy by nature, they prefer wooded areas or backyards thick with shrubs to give them plenty of cover.

EGG

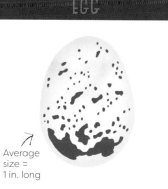

↗ Average size = 1 in. long

FUN FACT

The Carolina Wren scoots up and down tree trunks looking for insects in the bark.

ROH-ROH-ROH!

SIZE
Length: 38 to 54 inches
Wingspan: 66 to 80 inches

GREAT BLUE HERON

Ardea herodias

The Great Blue Heron is the largest heron in the United States. Their open wings span 6 feet! You won't find a Great Blue Heron in your backyard. They live near water and are not social with humans. It's best to observe these stately birds from a distance.

NEST

Great Blue Herons nest in colonies. That means many other herons are nearby, also busily building nests and preparing for hatchlings. They usually build their nests in trees, about 100 feet high. A male chooses the site and gathers materials like sticks, moss, and dry grass. The female then weaves the nest, which can be as large as 4 feet wide!

FOOD

They love to eat fish. They will stand very still in water, waiting for their next meal. When a fish swims by, they quickly spear the fish with their bill. They also eat insects, reptiles, small mammals, and even other birds. They're not picky!

■ YEAR-ROUND

HABITAT & RANGE

They live in freshwater and saltwater **habitats** all over the United States and Central America.

EGG

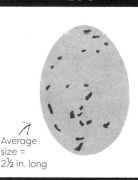

↗ Average size = 2½ in. long

FUN FACT

Great Blue Herons have excellent night vision. This helps them hunt after dark.

55

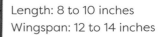

SIZE
Length: 8 to 10 inches
Wingspan: 12 to 14 inches

NORTHERN MOCKINGBIRD

Mimus polyglottos

HABITAT & RANGE

They live all over the United States. They prefer areas with shrubs, open spaces, and grass for **foraging,** like parks and suburban backyards.

These grayish-brown birds might seem a little boring at first glance. They don't have colorful feathers or striking features. But what they lack in color, they make up for in personality. The Northern Mockingbird is known to sing at all hours—even through the night!

NEST

Northern Mockingbirds most often build their nests in shrubs and trees, about 3 to 7 feet off the ground. The males will use twigs to build many nests. The female will then choose the nest it likes best and line it with grass, small roots, leaves, and trash.

FOOD

In the summer months, these birds will eat mostly insects, like butterflies, bees, and grasshoppers. In the fall and winter, they switch to eating mostly fruit. They enjoy all types of berries.

EGG

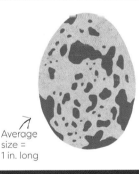

↗ Average size = 1 in. long

FUN FACT

The Northern Mockingbird sings different songs in different seasons!

KEE-EEEEE-ARR!

SIZE

Length: 17 to 26 inches
Wingspan: 45 to 52 inches

RED-TAILED HAWK

Buteo jamaicensis

If you've ever seen a hawk out the window of a car, it is most likely you have spotted the Red-Tailed Hawk. One of the largest birds in the United States, you can sometimes catch them soaring in circles in the sky.

NEST

These large birds build themselves very large nests. Usually around 6½ feet wide, they are most often built at the tops of tall trees or on cliffs.

FOOD

Red-Tailed Hawks eat mostly mammals, such as rabbits, rats, and squirrels. You won't be able to lure these birds to your bird feeder.

■ YEAR-ROUND

HABITAT & RANGE

They live in open **habitats** throughout the United States and in many types of environments, as long as they have tall places to perch and some open land for hunting.

EGG

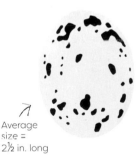

↗ Average size = 2½ in. long

FUN FACT

Female Red-Tailed Hawks are larger than males. This is rare in the animal world.

CHEK!

SIZE

Length: 5 to 5½ inches
Wingspan: 7½ to 9 inches

YELLOW-RUMPED WARBLER

Setophaga coronata

Depending on the season, the Yellow-Rumped Warbler will look slightly different. In the winter, they're streaked with dull shades of brown and yellow. But come spring, they **molt** and become much more colorful, with bright yellow, black, gray, and white feathers. They are known for **migrating** in huge numbers.

NEST

They build their nests in trees, between 4 and 50 feet high. The female uses pine needles, twigs, grass, and small roots for the cup-shaped nest. She then adds soft materials, such as feathers and hair.

FOOD

In the cooler months, they eat mostly fruits and wild seeds. In the warmer months, they eat a wide variety of insects, including a pest called the spruce budworm. This insect is a type of moth that destroys forests. These **warblers** help the forests by eating the insects.

YEAR-ROUND

HABITAT & RANGE

They live scattered over the United States, mostly in forests. Large numbers of Yellow-Rumped Warblers travel great distances in the spring and fall.

EGG

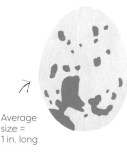

Average size = 1 in. long

FUN FACT

The Yellow-Rumped Warbler catches insects by swooping down from tree branches and catching them in midair!

COMMON GRACKLE

Quiscalus quiscula

You're likely to see the Common Grackle traveling in huge **flocks** with other blackbirds, starlings, and cowbirds. These social and intelligent birds have a striking appearance, with shiny feathers that seem to change color with the light.

NEST

The females choose the nesting site carefully. Sometimes they change their minds and start over somewhere else. The nest, which is made to be very sturdy, can take up to six weeks to build. It's made of twigs, grass, and leaves, then lined with mud, grass, and hair.

FOOD

Most of their diet comes from seeds, and they especially enjoy eating corn and rice. In the summer, about a quarter of their diet comes from animals, such as insects, frogs, fish, mice, and even other birds!

■ YEAR-ROUND

HABITAT & RANGE

They prefer to live in areas that offer a mix of trees and open ground. They are often found in suburbs and parks. It is common for grackles from the northern United States to travel to the central and southern United States for the winter months.

EGG

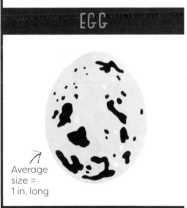

↗
Average size = 1 in. long

FUN FACT

Why does the Common Grackle let ants crawl all over it? The ants leave behind a substance called formic acid, which kills parasites!

63

CAROLINA CHICKADEE

Poecile carolinensis

The Carolina Chickadee is known for being cute, curious, friendly, and fun to watch. They are frequently confused with the Black-Capped Chickadee, which looks and sounds very similar. The best way to tell them apart? Look at a map! The Carolina Chickadee is found only in the southeastern United States.

NEST

Males and females work together to find a hole for their nest. The female then builds the nest, using moss, bark, hair, and plant parts.

FOOD

These birds eat mostly seeds, insects, and berries. In winter, they eat mostly seeds and berries, and in other months their diet has more insects. The main insect they eat is caterpillars.

■ **YEAR-ROUND**

HABITAT & RANGE

They live in forests and suburban yards and parks with large trees. They are found all over the southeastern United States.

EGG

Average size = ½ in. long

FUN FACT

The Carolina Chickadee is named for South Carolina, the state where it was first identified.

OINK!

SIZE

Length: 27½ to 35½ inches
Wingspan: 45 to 48½ inches

DOUBLE-CRESTED CORMORANT

Nannopterum auritum

The Double-Crested Cormorant is a sea bird known for its excellent diving skills. It can dive down to 150 feet in the water to catch small fish. It's named for the two tufts of feathers on its head. They can be hard to see when the bird is wet, making these birds sometimes hard to identify.

NEST

They build their nests high up in trees, perched over water, or on the ground near water. Their nests are made from sticks, seaweed, and grass. They have been known to steal materials from other nests to make their own!

FOOD

They eat mostly fish. They catch them by diving into the water and using their webbed feet to swim quickly. They have a hooked beak that helps them grab the fish.

HABITAT & RANGE

Found in just a few places across the United States, these are the birds you'd be most likely to see in freshwater. They live in groups in almost every kind of **aquatic habitat**.

EGG

↗
Average size = 2½ in. long

FUN FACT

The Double-Crested Cormorant's poop is called guano. When too much of it builds up, it can be deadly to trees.

RING-BILLED GULL

Larus delawarensis

If you've ever seen a large group of birds circling above a parking lot or garbage dump, there's a good chance you've spotted the Ring-Billed Gull. These medium-sized birds look for food around humans, and they're not shy about swooping down to grab a treat, even out of a person's hands!

NEST

The males and females build their nests together, usually on the ground. The nests are simple, made of twigs, sticks, leaves, and mosses. Nests tend to be reused for multiple seasons.

FOOD

They eat just about anything! They enjoy fish and insects, but will also eat fruit, such as blueberries and strawberries. If you spot a **flock**, keep your food guarded—they'll grab a french fry off your plate if you're not careful!

YEAR-ROUND

HABITAT & RANGE

Ring-Billed Gulls live throughout the United States but are found in a smaller location year-round. Unlike other types of gulls, they don't need to be by the ocean. They can be found by lakes, rivers, ponds, large parking lots, and landfills.

EGG

↗
Average size = 2½ in. long

FUN FACT

Ring-Billed Gulls can fly at speeds up to 40 miles per hour. They can also hover in the air, using the wind to help them stay airborne.

KILLDEER

Charadrius vociferus

The Killdeer is a type of shorebird that isn't usually found at the shore! They prefer open areas, like lawns and fields, where the plants are no taller than an inch. You may see them running and then stopping quickly. This is how they look for food.

NEST

Males and females make the nest together. The male will use its body to scrape the ground, creating a small dip in the earth. Only after eggs are laid will they start to add other materials, like rocks, sticks, and trash.

FOOD

You won't see Killdeer at your bird feeder, though they do eat seeds. They also eat some insects, such as earthworms, beetles, and grasshoppers.

YEAR-ROUND

HABITAT & RANGE

Killdeer are found all over the United States. They are often seen in open fields, like large lawns, parking lots, golf courses, and airports. Unlike other shorebirds, they don't need to live near water.

EGG

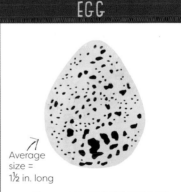

↗ Average size = 1½ in. long

FUN FACT

They are named for the sound they make when they're flying. The high pitched call sounds like "kill-deer!"

GRAY CATBIRD

Dumetella carolinensis

Gray Catbirds prefer to stay hidden among shrubbery, so the best way to spot them is to listen for them. They have a unique call that sounds like a cat's mew! These medium-sized birds are mostly gray, but they have a spot of black at the top of their heads and a brown patch under their tails.

NEST

The Gray Catbird builds its nest about 4 feet off the ground inside shrubs or in trees that are well hidden by greenery. The nest is usually made from twigs, straw, bark, and sometimes even trash. It is then lined with softer materials, like grass, hairs, and pine needles.

FOOD

In the summer, they eat insects, such as ants, beetles, caterpillars, and moths. In the cooler months, they look for fruit, such as cherries, blackberries, and elderberries.

■ **YEAR-ROUND**

HABITAT & RANGE

You can find Gray Catbirds across the United States in the warmer months. In the winter, they **migrate** to coastal areas in Texas and Florida and as far south as the Caribbean.

EGG

↗
Average size = 1 in. long

FUN FACT

You may be able to get a Gray Catbird to come to you by making a soft "pish" sound. Try it!

OH-SWEET-CANADA-CANADA!

SIZE

Length: 6 to 7 inches
Wingspan: 8 to 9 inches

WHITE-THROATED SPARROW

Zonotrichia albicollis

There are two types of this bird: tan-striped and white-striped. The white-striped birds are more colorful, with a bright yellow spot on their faces. The tan-striped birds are more of a dull brown color.

NEST

They like to build their nests underneath shrubbery or other plants that will keep the nests hidden. The female uses moss for the base and grass, twigs, bits of wood, and pine needles for the walls. Inside, she lines the nest with grasses, small roots, and deer hair.

FOOD

The White-Throated Sparrow eats seeds, like ragweed and buckwheat. They also eat fruits, like cranberries, blueberries, and sumac. In the cooler months, they feed on many types of insects, including dragonflies, stink bugs, and beetles. To attract them, include sunflower seeds and millet in your bird feeder.

YEAR-ROUND

HABITAT & RANGE

Most White-Throated Sparrows **migrate**. They're seen in parts of the far northern United States in the summer. In winter, they travel south, mostly to the northeastern and southeastern United States.

EGG

↗ Average size = 1 in. long

FUN FACT

The two different types of White-Throated Sparrows each have their own set of traits. The white-striped birds are known to be more aggressive. And the tan-striped birds are more caring.

75

I WARBLE!

SIZE

Length: 6 to 7½ inches
Wingspan: 11½ to 12½ inches

BARN SWALLOW

Hirundo rustica

When you first spot a Barn Swallow, you might be taken aback by its beauty! These graceful birds have unusual coloring, with a mix of glossy blue, black, orangish brown, and brick-red feathers. They don't usually eat from bird feeders, but you can encourage them to nest in your yard by providing them with mud for their nests.

NEST

Barn Swallows like to nest in buildings or other man-made structures, such as sheds or barns. To build their nests, they form a cup shape made of mud. Then they lay down grass and feathers. They are known to steal materials from other nests to make their own!

FOOD

Barn Swallows eat mostly flies. They also eat other insects, such as beetles, bees, and butterflies.

■ **BREEDING AND MIGRATION**

HABITAT & RANGE

Barn Swallows **breed** all over the United States, but year-round, you aren't able to see them in one place since they like to move a lot. They live in many different **habitats** that have large grassy areas to look for food.

EGG

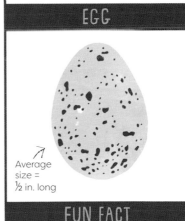

↗ Average size = ½ in. long

FUN FACT

Barn Swallow parents get help from young birds to care for their **nestlings**. It takes a village!

CHIP!

SIZE

Length: 5 to 6 inches
Wingspan: 8 inches

CHIPPING SPARROW

Spizella passerina

It is easier to identify the Chipping Sparrow in the summer. The feathers on its head are rust-colored and the black line beside the eye is crisp. These little sparrows are often found near humans. If you have a yard with trees and some open space, there's a good chance you will spot them!

NEST

Females build the nest. They usually choose a spot in a tree or shrub, between 3 and 10 feet high. The nest is a loose cup shape made up of small roots and grasses, lined with animal hair and thin plant strips.

FOOD

They eat different types of seeds, insects, and sometimes small fruits, like cherries. To attract them to your yard, offer millet in a bird feeder or scattered on the ground.

■ **YEAR-ROUND**

HABITAT & RANGE

Chipping Sparrows live all over the United States. You can find them in areas that have a mix of trees and open areas, like grassy forests, parks, and large backyards. Look for them in evergreen trees—a Chipping Sparrow's favorite.

EGG

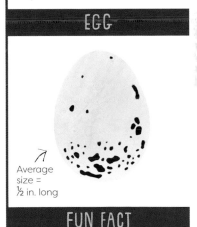

↗
Average size = ½ in. long

FUN FACT

It is not uncommon for the Brown-Headed Cowbird to lay a single egg in a Chipping Sparrow's nest.

TU-A-WEE!

SIZE

Length: 6 to 8 inches
Wingspan: 10 to 12½ inches

EASTERN BLUEBIRD

Sialia sialis

Eastern Bluebirds are prized for their beautiful coloring and sweet personalities. Spending much of their time perched on branches and posts, they use their fantastic eyesight to spot insects on the ground. If you want to attract them to your yard, add mealworms to your bird feeder!

NEST

They look for holes and spaces in trees and other structures to make nests. The female builds the nest by weaving grasses and pine needles, then lines it with grass and sometimes hair and feathers.

FOOD

Most of the year, they eat insects, such as caterpillars, crickets, and grasshoppers. In the cooler months, they also eat a lot of fruit, such as blueberries, and juniper berries. Occasionally they will prey on larger animals, like lizards, snakes, and frogs.

■ **YEAR-ROUND**

HABITAT & RANGE

They live mostly in the eastern and central United States. They live in open areas, like parks, suburban backyards, and golf courses.

EGG

↗
Average size = 1 in. long

FUN FACT

If you want to draw Eastern Bluebirds to your yard, leave out nest boxes for them. Nest boxes are small wooden boxes left out for birds to build nests in. Birdhouses are a type of nest box.

BROWN-HEADED COWBIRD

Molothrus ater

The Brown-Headed Cowbird has a very unusual way of reproducing. Instead of building a nest and having the female lay eggs there, this bird lays her eggs in the nests of other birds! In doing so, she can lay many more eggs in a **breeding** season, sometimes as many as three dozen!

NEST

Because cowbirds lay their eggs in nests of other birds, the hatchlings that survive are raised alongside totally different types of birds.

FOOD

They mostly eat seeds and some grains. They also eat a fair amount of insects, such as grasshoppers and beetles. To attract them to your yard, try adding grain to bird feeders or scattering it on the ground.

YEAR ROUND

HABITAT & RANGE

They live all throughout the United States. They **migrate** short distances for the summer and winter. You can find them in grasslands, fields, and towns with lots of open land.

EGG

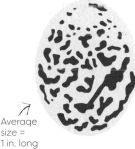

↗ Average size = 1 in. long

FUN FACT

Cowbirds are known to **forage** in pastures, following cows to eat the insects they leave behind. That's how they got their name!

SONG!

SIZE

Length: 4½ to 6 inches
Wingspan: 12 to 14 inches

TREE SWALLOW

Tachycineta bicolor

These pretty little **songbirds** are especially fun to watch in flight. They soar, dive, dip, and glide with graceful flaps of their wings. Adult males are very colorful. Females and the very young have duller brown feathers.

NEST

They build their nests in empty spaces of dead trees, holes left by woodpeckers, and nesting boxes. The female builds the nest, usually from just grass, but sometimes with pine needles, animal hair, and other materials. She presses her body to the nest to form the shape.

FOOD

While soaring through the air, they gobble up flying insects, such as damselflies, true bugs, and moths. They spend all day looking for food, usually flying no farther than 40 feet off the ground.

■ **BREEDING AND MIGRATION**

HABITAT & RANGE

You can find Tree Swallows throughout the United States, however, they can't be spotted in one place year-round. Many **migrate** long distances from the northern United States to the southern United States and Central America in the cold months.

EGG

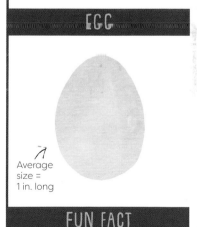

↗
Average size = 1 in. long

FUN FACT

During the **breeding** season, Tree Swallows may search for eggshells in compost bins. These give them the extra calcium they need to make their eggs.

85

COO-OO!

SIZE

Length: 12 to 14 inches
Wingspan: 20 to 26½ inches

ROCK PIGEON

Columba livia

■ YEAR-ROUND

Often seen in a **flock** with other pigeons, these medium-sized birds spend much of their time looking for food. They walk or run while pecking at the ground, picking up seeds as they go. Rock Pigeons are known to fly away when startled—keep still if you want to watch them!

HABITAT & RANGE

They live throughout the United States in towns and urban areas. You can often see large flocks at city parks, where they peck at scraps from humans.

NEST

Males choose the nesting spot and coo to attract a mate. Once paired, the female will build the nest out of materials the male brings her, usually straw, stems, and sticks. They will reuse this nest many times.

EGG

↗
Average size = 1½ in long

FOOD

They are not picky eaters. In the wild, they eat seeds and fruit and they will also peck at any food garbage left behind.

FUN FACT

These pigeons drink by dipping their beaks in water and sucking through it like a straw!

COMMON YELLOWTHROAT

Geothlypis trichas

The Common Yellowthroat can be hard to spot. It spends a lot of time looking for food on the ground, hidden by shrubbery. The best way to see one is to look out for its jerky way of flying and listen for its unique song.

NEST

The female finds the nesting site and builds the nest. She usually chooses a place on or near the ground. The nest is made from mostly grasses and leaves. They sometimes build their nests with roofs!

FOOD

Common Yellowthroats look for food on the ground and on low plants. They eat many different types of insects, including termites, bees, and dragonflies.

■ **YEAR-ROUND**

HABITAT & RANGE

They are found all over the United States in many **habitats**, including forests and suburban yards. Most Common Yellowthroats **migrate**, but some in the southern United States stay put year-round.

EGG

↗
Average size = ½ in. long

FUN FACT

Only the adult male Common Yellowthroats have a black mask. They can tell whether other yellowthroats are male or female based on whether or not they have it.

MY BIRD LOG

Here you can keep track of all the birds you have spotted. In the Notes column, add details about the bird's appearance or behavior.

NAME OF BIRD	DATE	LOCATION	NOTES

NAME OF BIRD	DATE	LOCATION	NOTES
			91

CONSERVATION

Birds are fun to watch and study! But it's important to remember that birds are not just fun, but also very important to our planet. We count on birds to act as a natural pest control, eating many insects and rodents. We also depend on birds to spread pollen, which helps plants grow. We need a variety of plants in order to stay healthy.

**So how can you help protect
the birds? There's lots you can do
in your own backyard:**

→ Consider adding plants that will attract birds or
nest boxes to give them places to build a safe nest.

→ Choose food for your bird feeder carefully,
making sure to add foods that are preferred by birds
in your area.

→ Keep your pet cats inside! Outdoor cats are
predators to many types of birds. Cats kill billions of
birds every year.

→ Do some research about natural pesticides
and talk to your family about ways to avoid using
chemicals that are dangerous to birds.

→ Do what you can to stop climate change.
Recycling, limiting gasoline usage, and saving
electricity are all helpful steps.

You can also share your love of birding with others.
The more people are interested in helping birds, the
better! Offer to take a friend or family member on a
bird walk and show them what you've learned. Teach
others about the importance of birds and spread the
news about why we need them.

GLOSSARY

aquatic   Having to do with water.

breeding   Producing offspring.

carrion   The flesh of a dead animal.

crest   A tuft of feathers that forms a point on the top of a bird's head.

crop   A pouch that some birds have in their throat where they can store food.

flock   A group of birds.

foliage   A grouping of leaves, flowers, and branches.

forage   To search for food.

habitat   The environment or place where an animal naturally lives.

migrate   The act of moving from one place to another. Birds usually migrate during the summer and winter months.

molting   When feathers fall out and new ones grow.

nestling   A young bird that still lives in the nest.

range   Locations across the United States where you can spot birds during these phases: year-round, migration, breeding, and nonbreeding.

songbird   A type of bird that is known for its musical singing.

suet   A type of beef fat often used in bird food.

warbler   A type of bird that is usually tiny and brightly colored.

woodland   An area of land covered with trees.

First Edition
27 26 25 24 23   6 5 4 3 2

Published by Gibbs Smith
P.O. Box 667 Layton, Utah 84041
1.800.835.4993 orders
www.gibbs-smith.com

Designed by Virginia Snow and Nicole LaRue

Manufactured in China June 2023 by RR Donnelley Asia Printing Solutions.

Gibbs Smith books are printed on either recycled, 100% post-consumer waste, FSC-certified papers or on paper produced from a 100% certified sustainable forest/controlled wood source.

Library of Congress Cataloging-in-Publication Data

Names: Berkowitz, Eliza, author. | LaRue, Nicole, illustrator.
Title: A kid's guide to backyard birds / Eliza Berkowitz, Nicole LaRue.
Description: First edition. | Layton : Gibbs Smith, 2023.
Identifiers: LCCN 2022029072 (print) | LCCN 2022029073 (ebook) | ISBN 9781423662631 (paperback) | ISBN 9781423662648 (ebook)
Subjects: LCSH: Birds—United States—Identification—Juvenile literature. | Bird watching—United States—Handbooks, manuals, etc.—Juvenile literature. | LCGFT: Field guides.
Classification: LCC QL682 .B47 2023 (print) | LCC QL682 (ebook) | DDC 598.072/34—dc23/eng/20220713